When My Autism Gets Too Big!

A Relaxation Book for Children
with Autism Spectrum Disorders

Written and Illustrated
by Kari Dunn Buron

Foreword by Brenda Smith Myles

When My Autism Gets Too Big!

A Relaxation Book for Children with Autism Spectrum Disorders

Written and Illustrated
by Kari Dunn Buron

AAPC

Autism Asperger Publishing Company
P.O. Box 23173
Shawnee Mission, Kansas 66283-0173
www.asperger.net

Foreword by Brenda Smith Myles

© 2003 by Autism Asperger Publishing Company
P.O. Box 23173
Shawnee Mission, Kansas 66283-0173
www.asperger.net

Buron, Kari Dunn.
    When my autism gets too big! / by Kari Dunn Buron. –
    p. cm.
    SUMMARY: Presents ways for young children with autism
spectrum disorders to recognize when they are losing
control and constructive ways to deal with it.
    Audience: Ages 5-9.
    ISBN: 1-931282-51-X
    Library of Congress Control Number: 2003110482

    1. Autism–Juvenile literature. 2. Autism in
children–Juvenile literature. [1. Autism. 2. Autism in
children.] I. Title.

RC553.A88B87 2003   616.89'82
                                     QBI33-1438

Managing Editor: Kirsten McBride
Interior Design/Production: Tappan Design and Eddy Mora

Printed in the United States of America

This book is dedicated to
Nicholas, Jamie, Mary, Tony,
Melanie and Mo, who
inspired me to keep trying.

Foreword

Children and youth with Asperger Syndrome, high-functioning autism, and autism (collectively referred to as autism spectrum disorders, ASD) are complex because they have a multifaceted disability that manifests itself differently within each individual. In short, if you have seen one child with ASD, you have seen one child with ASD. The next child with ASD you work or live with may look or act completely differently!

This unique individuality presents challenges to teachers, parents, and researchers attempting to develop interventions that consistently address the needs inherent in the exceptionality but are flexible enough to be used with many children. Partnered with this task is the need for interventions that can be implemented without an extensive time investment (because there is never enough time at home or at school) and that can be used in both general and special education environments as well as in homes and communities. Not many interventions have been able to meet these demanding requirements.

Every once in a while an intervention comes across my desk that meets these criteria. *When My Autism Gets Too Big!* is one such gift to the ASD community. This structured yet flexible, child- and adult-friendly intervention can be used in many environments. In this charming book, Kari Dunn Buron, whose years of experience with individuals with ASD truly make her an expert, has addressed some of the biggest challenges experienced by many of our children and youth—the inability to self-monitor stress, the rapid escalation from worry to meltdowns, and problems knowing how to relax or return to a state of calmness. Kari refers to these situations as "when autism gets too big." Used generically in this book, *autism* refers to the quick escalation to meltdowns experienced by individuals across the spectrum.

This book is intended to help children with ASD understand that sometimes their autism does get too big and that they are not alone in this challenge. To make this more concrete, Kari rates the "bigness of autism" on a 5-point scale, with a rating of "1" meaning little or no stress and a rating of "5" referring to the stage when the autism is "way too big" and may result in a meltdown. She empowers children by telling them that they can fight back against the "bigness of autism" and take control in trying to return to or remain in a calm state.

Teachers and parents can use this book to help children with ASD identify their behavior at each of the five stages and remember things they can do if their autism gets too big. The book opens with Nicholas, who talks about how children with autism can be very intelligent and do things well. He asks the reader to identify what he does well in a drawing or in writing. Nicholas then introduces the first stage of autism, "1," explaining that a "1" feeling is one of relaxation and enjoyment. He also identifies other things that help people with autism feel they are at a "1," such as being reassured by knowing what will happen next. Nicholas then works readers through the various stages and asks them to indicate in illustrations and/or writing what makes them feel as if they are at a "5." He introduces several strategies that children and youth with ASD can use to get back to a "1" and asks them to draw and identify their own relaxation strategies. This exercise helps turn the abstract concept of tantrums, rage, and meltdowns into something concrete and personal. Teachers and parents, by reading the book with children with ASD, help them understand their behavior and its cause.

To add to the tremendous benefits of this book, a 5-point thermometer is introduced at the end that the teacher and child can complete to identify behaviors at each stage and what the child can do to help himself feel like his autism is at a "1." This simple thermometer is brilliant. It places on one small piece of paper everything about the "bigness of autism" for a particular child. The child can have the thermometer on her desk or velcroed inside her textbook or notebook for easy reference throughout the day.

The applicability of this strategy is broad. I envision a child with ASD who has used Kari's book in a general education class. He has a thermometer on his desk and the teacher carries a duplicate on the back of her I.D. badge. When she looks to the child periodically, she discreetly turns her badge around to silently ask the child how big his autism is. He points to his thermometer in response; they smile knowingly at each other.

When My Autism Gets Too Big! is a wonderful book. It is a simple-to-use strategy that can help children and youth with ASD be successful. Children who use this book will find themselves relaxed and ready to work or play. In Kari's words, children with ASD will realize that "They are awesome and in control!"

Thank you, Kari, for this brilliant and easy-to-use intervention!

— Brenda Smith Myles, Ph.D.

Autism Syndrome and Difficult Moments: Practical Solutions for Tantrums, Rage, and Meltdowns, Asperger Syndrome and Sensory Issues: Practical Solutions for Making Sense of the World, and *Asperger Syndrome and Adolescence: Practical Solutions for School Success*

Dear Parents and Teachers,

High levels of stress and anxiety related to social situations, sensory issues or general frustration are common in children with autism spectrum disorders (ASD). Such stress can lead to a loss of control, resulting in aggressive behavior such as screaming, throwing things or even hurting someone. More than any other issue for students with ASD, loss of control can lead to the need to move them out of the general education classroom to a more restrictive educational environment equipped to deal with behavior challenges. Sometimes this means a special room at school; sometimes it means a special program outside of the neighborhood school. Even when children are able to stay in the general education classroom, peers are more likely to avoid children who "explode" without warning. Therefore, it is critical that we help children with ASD learn to control their feelings.

Those of us who teach and live with children with ASD are often so focused on teaching them other things that we forget that teaching someone to relax can benefit them in the long term more than any other skill.

Although I have not found many books on how to teach relaxation to children, a few resources have been helpful to me. For example, the Groden Center in Rhode Island has been working on progressive relaxation with children with developmental disabilities for many years (www.grodencenter.com). I have also found the book *A Boy and a Bear: The Children's Relaxation Book* (Lori Lite, 1998) to be wonderful for introducing relaxation to children.

When My Autism Gets Too Big! is based on cognitive behavioral management, which is an approach to behavior management that focuses on teaching children to recognize their own feelings of anxiety and then teaching them strategies to help them control those feelings. I got the idea for the book when working with a kindergarten student named Nicholas, who had difficulty tolerating the everyday surprises that school offers, such as when the daily schedule was interrupted to fit in a school assembly or when a substitute came for the day. Originally, I taught Nicholas a relaxation routine we called "Relaxed Body"—a routine inspired by my friend Joyce Santo, who had been teaching her four- and five-year-old students with autism to complete a relaxation routine prior to stressful events.

"Relaxed Body" went something like this:
1. Take three long breaths.
2. Stretch your arms up over your head, down and up again.
3. Rub your hands together and count to 3.
4. Rub your thighs and count to 3.
5. Take another long breath.

My experience with Nicholas impressed upon me that a highly anxious five-year-old was capable of learning the first steps to relaxation. After hearing about the routine, Nicholas' teacher asked him to teach it to the whole class, and later commented that it seemed like a logical thing to teach all young children.

Nicholas loved to create books about his special interests (we often created stories about sprinklers and water towers), so I decided to use his interest in creating books to increase his willingness to participate in the task. In addition to relaxation, the book also introduced the concept of visualization and attempted to add some humor to an otherwise difficult task. I also decided to incorporate a 5-point scale to define different levels of stress. The numbers seem to make it easier for children to understand their feelings.

When reading this book with a child, talk about the child's feelings in terms of numbers to help her sort out the difference between just being excited because something is fun (being at a 3) and falling into the 4 range, where the child may feel he is losing control. This book gives children the opportunity to label their own levels 1-5 and share how each level feels. Teaching relaxation is a long process but can be extremely helpful. I hope you find this book useful in the process.

— Kari

I have autism and that
can be a good thing.
Some kids with autism are really
good at their favorite things.

I am really good at

_____

_____

Here I am doing my favorite thing.

When I am thinking about my
favorite things,
I am <u>so</u> relaxed.
My autism is at a **1** or **2**.

When I know what is going to happen or I really like what I am doing, I am most definitely at a **1** or **2**.

But sometimes I worry too much, like
when I first get on the bus and
I don't know where to sit.

When I worry too much, my autism is at a **4**. Sometimes a **4** makes my stomach hurt.

Sometimes I worry way too much,
like when I think I am going to recess
and it gets canceled!

This might make me scream or even hit someone. This is a **5**. Now my autism is TOO BIG!

One thing that makes
my autism too big is

_____

_____

Here I am
at a ⑤
⬇

This is when I need to fight back!
First, I can squeeze my hands together.

Next, I can take three really slow, deep breaths. Slow in – slow out, slow in – slow out, slow in – slow out.

Then I can sit down,
rub my legs and close
my eyes. Now I feel more
like a **3** or a **2**.

I can think about happy things,
like my dog or my stuffed lion, or our
family cabin in the summer.
Now I am at a **1**.

Here are some things
that I can think about to help me
bring a **5** feeling down to a **1** feeling.

You can do other things
to help you relax.
You can go for a walk,
go to your bedroom,
or go to a safe place at school.

Here I am relaxed and ready to work.
I am at a **1**, feeling good
and feeling proud!

Let me tell you about my autism
(How does it look? What does it feel like?)

5

4

3

2

1

7083